DR. BOB'S
AMAZING WORLD OF
ANIMALS
WARTHOGS

By Ruth Owen

WINDMILL
BOOKS
New York

Published in 2014 by Windmill Books, An Imprint of Rosen Publishing
29 East 21st Street, New York, NY 10010

Editor for Ruby Tuesday Books Ltd: Mark J. Sachner
US Editor: Joshua Shadowens
Designer: Trudi Webb

Photo Credits: Cover, 1, 4–5, 6–7, 8–9, 10–11, 12–13, 14–15, 18–19, 21, 22–23, 24–25, 26–27, 28–29, 30 © Shutterstock; 16–17 © FLPA; 20 © Didier Descouens.

Library of Congress Cataloging-in-Publication Data

Owen, Ruth.
 Warthogs / by Ruth Owen.
     pages cm. — (Dr. Bob's amazing world of animals)
 Includes index.
 ISBN 978-1-47779-044-1 (library) — ISBN 978-1-47779-045-8 (pbk.) —
 ISBN 978-1-47779-046-5 (6-pack)
 1. Warthog—Juvenile literature. I. Title.
 QL737.U58.O94 2014
 599.63'3—dc23
                                    2013027433
Manufactured in the United States of America

CPSIA Compliance Information: Batch #BW14WM: For Further Information contact Windmill Books, New York, New York at 1-866-478-0556

Contents

The Warthog

Welcome to my amazing world of animals. Today, we are visiting grassy **savannas** in Africa to find out about warthogs.

Tusk

A warthog

Let's investigate...

Hank's
WOOF OF WISDOM!

Warthogs are a type of pig. They are the wild cousins of pigs that are raised on farms.

It's easy to guess where the warthog's name came from. These wild pigs, or hogs, have large, wart-like growths of thick skin on their faces.

Warts

A male warthog is called a boar. A female warthog is called a sow. Baby warthogs are called piglets.

Land of the Warthog

The savanna **habitat** of the warthog is hot and dry for most of the year.

The areas marked in orange are where warthogs can be found.

Europe

Africa

Atlantic
Ocean

Indian
Ocean

When rain falls on the savanna it refills the pools and water holes that the savanna animals use for drinking and bathing.

Water hole

Savannas are open places covered with grass and plants. Trees grow on savannas, but unlike in a forest, there is lots of space between each tree.

Warthog Bodies

Warthogs have large heads and snouts and **sturdy** bodies.

These wild pigs have very tough skin. Their bodies have a thin covering of hair.

Mane

A warthog has a thick mane of hair on its back.

Warthog Size Chart

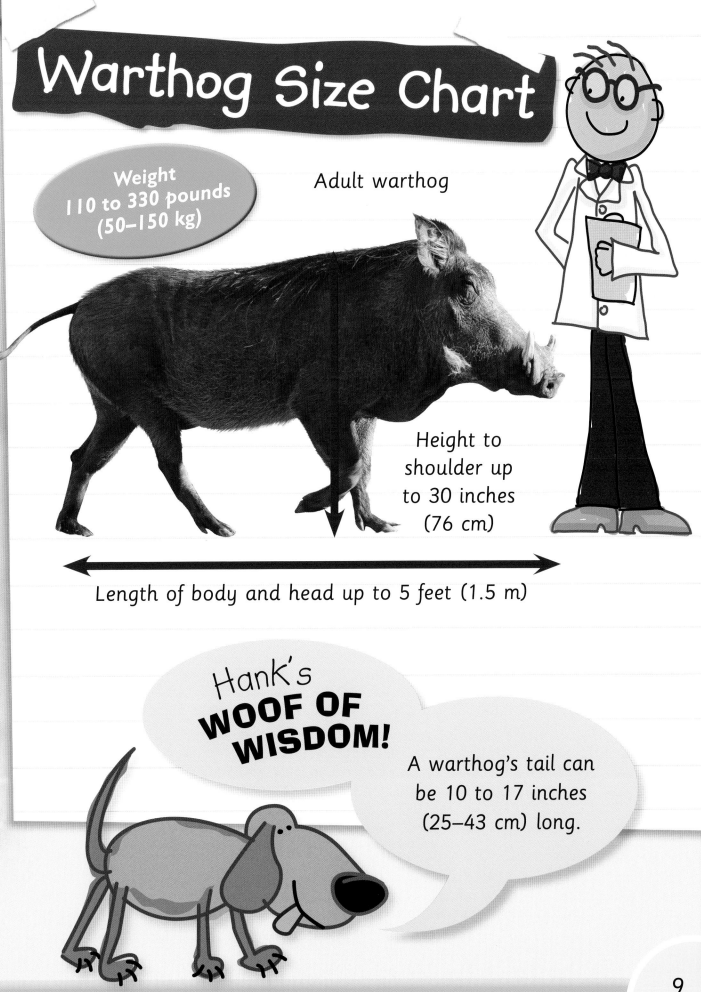

Weight
110 to 330 pounds
(50–150 kg)

Adult warthog

Height to shoulder up to 30 inches (76 cm)

Length of body and head up to 5 feet (1.5 m)

Hank's
WOOF OF WISDOM!

A warthog's tail can be 10 to 17 inches (25–43 cm) long.

Warthog Families

Female warthogs and their piglets live in groups called **sounders**.

There may be up to 40 warthogs in a sounder. The warthogs in the group are often related to each other. So a female might live with her mother and sisters.

A warthog sounder uses squeals, chirrups, snorts, grunts, and growls to communicate with each other.

Adult female warthog

Male warthogs usually live alone. They only join a group when it is the time of year for them to **mate** with females.

Warthog piglets

What's on the Menu?

Warthogs mostly eat plants, but they will sometimes eat worms, insects, or dead animals that they find on the savanna.

Warthogs graze on grass and eat berries and tree bark. They also use their snouts, and sometimes tusks, to dig for food. Warthogs dig up and eat underground plant parts such as roots and **bulbs**.

A warthog's tough, padded front knees allow it to kneel down while eating grass or digging for food.

Often warthogs shuffle from place to place on their front knees as they **forage** for food.

Bath Time

When the Sun gets too hot on the savanna, there's only one way to cool off. Take a bath!

A warthog will find a water hole and submerge its body in the water.

Warthogs also like to spend time wallowing in mud.

Water and mud don't just cool off a warthog's hot skin. While the animal is taking its bath, insects can't get to its body and give it painful bites!

A Warthog's Home

Warthogs spend most of their day looking for food and eating. At night, they sleep in burrows in the ground.

A warthog backs into its burrow, and then its large head blocks the entrance. The hog's sharp tusks scare off any animals that might disturb it while it rests.

Hank's
WOOF OF WISDOM!

Warthogs don't dig their own burrows. They use natural holes in the ground or move into empty burrows that once belonged to other animals, especially aardvarks.

HANK'S HOME

Burrow

The temperature inside an underground burrow stays the same all the time.

By day, when the Sun is at its hottest, it is cool underground. At night, it can be very cold on the savanna. Inside a warthog's burrow, however, it is warm and cozy.

Warthog Enemies

Warthogs share their habitat with many large hunters. Lions, leopards, cheetahs, hyenas, and wild dogs all eat warthogs.

Warthogs might look like tough fighters, but if a **predator** comes near, they will usually run away. A warthog can run at up to 30 miles per hour (48 km/h).

Hyenas

LOOK OUT DANGER!

Hank's WOOF OF WISDOM!

When a warthog runs, it holds its tail upright with the tuft on the end hanging down. Scientists think that the position of the animal's tail might be a warning to other warthogs that danger is near.

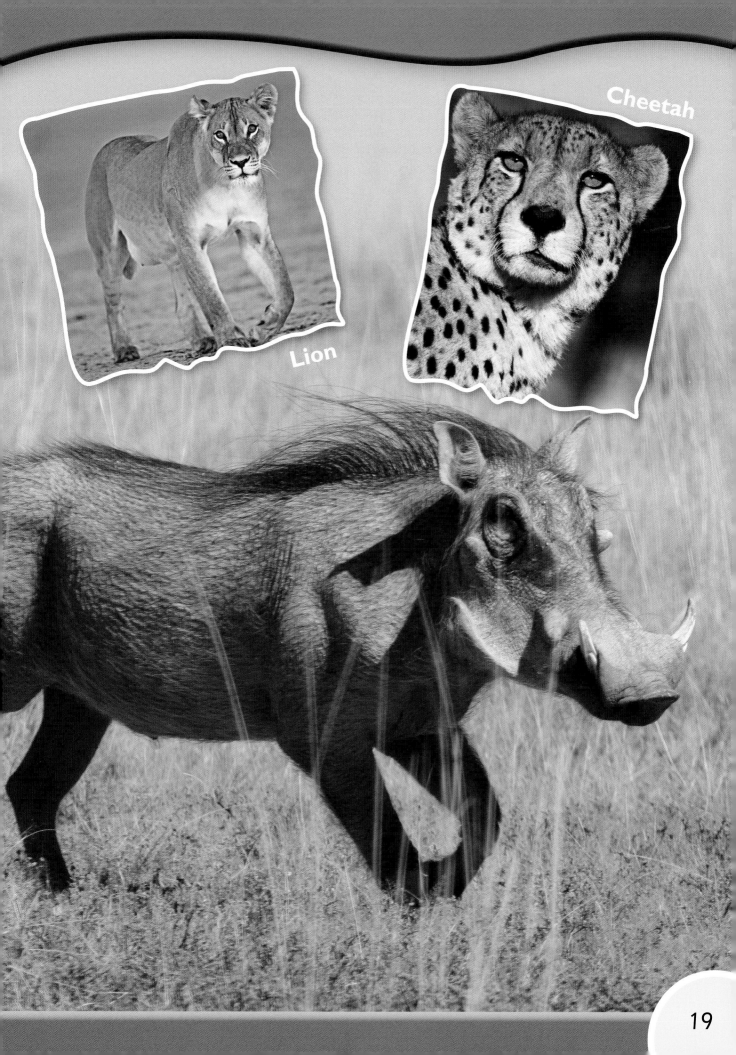

Lion

Cheetah

Tough Tusks

When chased by a predator, a warthog will sometimes run to its burrow and speedily back itself in.

Once a warthog is in its burrow, an enemy has to decide if it's worth attacking and risking getting hurt by the warthog's tusks.

Warthog skull

The curved upper tusks of an old warthog might be 2 feet (61 cm) long.

Upper tusk

A warthog's sharp lower tusks can grow to 6 inches (15 cm) long.

Lower tusk

Warthogs are good at running and dodging predators. If an enemy corners a warthog, however, it fights back with its tusks.

Getting the Girls

When it is time for warthogs to mate, males sometimes fight over females.

One male will run at his opponent so that the heads of the two fighters clash. The fighting males battle with their heads and upper tusks.

Finally the weaker warthog gives in and walks away. The winning fighter gets the girl!

Tough warthogs may fight hard, but neither animal usually gets hurt.

The thick, warty lumps on the animals' faces may act as pads to help protect their heads during fights.

Warthog Piglets

About six months after mating, a female warthog is ready to give birth.

The pregnant sow leaves her sounder to be alone. She finds a burrow where she can give birth to her piglets, safe from predators.

Warthog piglet

A newborn warthog piglet weighs 1 to 2 pounds (454–907 g).

There are usually one to four warthog piglets in a litter. The mother warthog feeds them with milk from her body.

Little Warthogs

For the first six to seven weeks of the piglets' lives, the little warthogs do not leave the burrow.

The mother warthog goes outside to forage. Then she returns to the burrow to feed her babies.

Mother warthog

Piglets

Once the piglets leave the burrow, they follow their mother everywhere.

Piglets drinking milk

If a predator comes close, the family runs back to their burrow. The piglets dive in head first. Then the mother warthog backs in, blocking the entrance.

Growing Up

Warthog piglets start to eat grass and other plants in their first couple of months.

The piglets drink their mother's milk until they are about six months old.

A warthog becomes an adult when it is about 20 months old. At this age, a young female is ready to have piglets of her own.

Young male warthogs start mating when they are about four years old. Until this time, they are not strong enough to fight with older, bigger males.

Glossary

bulbs (BUHLBZ) Round, underground parts of some plants. A bulb stores food for the plant that is growing above ground.

forage (FOR-ij) Search for food.

habitat (HA-buh-tat) The place where an animal or plant normally lives. A habitat may be a forest, the ocean, or a backyard.

mate (MAYT) When a male and female animal get together to produce young.

predator (PREH-duh-tur) An animal that hunts and kills other animals for food.

savannas (suh-VA-nuhz) Areas of land covered in grasses and other plants. Trees grow on savannas but they are not close together as in a forest. Some savannas are hot and dry, while others are hot and moist.

sturdy (STUR-dee) Strong and well built.

Dr. Bob's Fast Fact Board

During times when no rain falls, a warthog can survive without drinking water for several months.

Oxpecker birds often ride on warthogs. The birds help the hogs by eating ticks and insects that bite the warthogs.

Warthogs live between 12 and 18 years.

There are large numbers of warthogs living wild in Africa. At the moment, these animals are not endangered.

Websites

For web resources related to the subject of this book, go to:

www.windmillbooks.com/weblinks

and select this book's title.

Read More

Borgert-Spaniol, Megan. *Warthogs*. Animal Safari. Minneapolis, MN: Bellwether Media, 2012.

Ottina, Laura. *On the Savanna*. Learn With Animals. New York: Gareth Stevens, 2009.

Reade, Clara. *Warthogs*. PowerKids Readers: Safari Animals. New York: PowerKids Press, 2012.

Index